God GOES ON VACATION

Text and illustrations by Edwina Gateley

Paulist Press
New York/Mahwah, NJ

Cover and book design by Lynn Else

Text and illustrations copyright © 1994, 2009 by Edwina Gateley
God's Favorite Recipe: Peanut Dreams by Kelly Clarke

Library of Congress Cataloging-in-Publication Data

Gateley, Edwina.
    God goes on vacation / text and illustrations by Edwina Gateley.
        p. cm.
    Summary: While God is on vacation at the beach, the people of the world find the God-magic in their own hearts and discover how to do good on their own.
    ISBN 978-0-8091-6747-0 (alk. paper)
    [1. God—Fiction. 2. Vacations—Fiction. 3. Beaches—Fiction.] I. Title.
    PZ7.G2158Go 2009
    [E]—dc22
                                                                2008044051

Paulist Press
997 Macarthur Boulevard
Mahwah, New Jersey 07430

www.paulistpress.com

Printed and bound in the
United States of America

DEDICATION

For my son, Niall Kizito, who first inspired this book,

And for children throughout the world.

May they come to know a God who is not limited

By gender, color, and our small vision of life,

But who is big enough and free enough

To transcend all, and to be all.

God was very tired. Every day and every hour and every minute, and even every second, children and grown-ups were lining up at God's cloud with all sorts of questions and problems.

Even though he loved everybody and always helped them, God wished people would sometimes believe in their own inside magic. Poor God just never got a break.

Then one very rainy day, just as God was telling yet another little boy not to worry about his puppy who was lost, God got a great idea. "I'll take a vacation!" God said.

God was very excited and telephoned Stardrop, an angel, who also needed a vacation. They looked at all the world to decide where to go. "Let's go to the beach!" said Stardrop. God thought that was a wonderful idea and they started packing right away.

This is what God and Stardrop packed:

1 Swimsuit
1 Pair of swimming trunks
2 Beach hats
2 Towels
3 Pairs of sunglasses
   (in case one got broken)
Sunscreen
Lots of books
Some paints
A box of shells

Stardrop also packed a big picnic basket with God's favorite food, peanut dreams, and some soda and some celery sticks.

God put a big notice on the door. It read: GONE TO THE BEACH. Then God wrote another note for all the children and grown-ups who would come to the door, telling them he had left some of his special magic in each of their hearts.

This magic in their hearts was like having a little bit of God inside them, so they would never really be alone. The little bit of God-magic, which each one had hidden inside them, could help them be everything they wanted to be and to do all sorts of things!

God and Stardrop flew to Florida.

They had such fun. On the first day, God decided to be a lady God, because God can do anything and be lots of different things. God wore a big yellow sun hat and looked great. She played with all the children just like you would expect a mother God to play and have fun. God also made friends with a red crab who was called Clarissa, and a spider called Samantha.

On the second day, God was brown and ran on the beach in a new jogging suit. He met a friendly worm called Wentworth, who liked to be called "Sir Wentworth Worm." This was because of the special work God had given him to do, wiggling through the soil on the earth, making it rich and fertile. So Sir Wentworth Worm felt important and always wore a crown.

God felt FREE.
He wished that all children and grown-ups knew they were free too.
It made God very happy just to think about it. But God knew that for people to be free, they would have to help each other and be very kind to each other.

On the third day, God was a beautiful black color and went waterskiing with Stardrop. They took turns driving the boat. God wore a shiny blue water suit and fell only twice. God thought: "It's okay not to make it every time!"

An octopus called Octavius waved his eight legs to God as he sped past. Samantha Spider waved all her eight legs too. Everyone got wet—even Sir Wentworth Worm, who was in God's pocket.

On the fourth day, God was a lady again and danced all the way down the beach for an ice cream. God wished all the children in the world could have ice cream. Of course, people would have to share a lot more for that to happen.

On the fifth day, God and Stardrop made sand castles. God wore a crisp new Arab dress, because Arabs know all about sand in their country. Sir Wentworth Worm and Clarissa Crab played too. Samantha Spider played "swing" from God's bucket.

God enjoyed imagining what it was like to be in different countries and to do things in different ways.

Right at the beginning of the world, God was so excited about making everybody, that he made them in many colors and gave them many languages. That's what makes the world such a beautiful place. It's fun to explore and to get to know all kinds of people and countries.

On the sixth day it rained, so God stayed in the hotel thinking about himself, while Stardrop went shopping. God enjoyed a bit of quiet time. God knew it was good to be alone sometimes just to think and listen to the raindrops falling and the wind blowing.

On the seventh day, God and Stardrop packed to go home. God was very, very happy, and very well rested.

But back on the beach, God's new friends were not so happy.

Sir Wentworth Worm, Samantha Spider, and Clarissa Crab all wanted to go to heaven with God and Stardrop. Octavius needed to practice some more swimming strokes and asked if he could come later. God said, "Okay, heaven is for everybody."

God never left out anybody or anything.

So off they all went.
Up...up...up into God's beautiful sky.
Past the clouds, past the sun, past the moon, past the stars, to the special place where God listens to everybody's heart.

When God and Stardrop, Sir Wentworth Worm, Clarissa Crab, and Samantha Spider arrived, they found lots and lots of children and grown-ups dancing around God's cloud. There was great excitement.

Everyone was cheering God. It was obvious they were feeling very happy and free. They all shouted and did lots of other happy things, which made God feel really good. Sir Wentworth Worm wiggled in excitement.

Everyone had found the God-magic in their hearts. When they found the God-magic, they knew that they could be strong and do good things. Even though God was on vacation, God was with them as well. WOW!

The children and even the grown-ups knew that they didn't need to be afraid again because God was always with them. They just needed to know that and take care of each other. That was the magic they had found!

God was very, very happy that he had taken a vacation. So were Sir Wentworth Worm, Samantha Spider, and Clarissa Crab. Stardrop showed her three new friends around heaven and welcomed them to Spider Superdome, Worm Wonderland, and Crab Cove. WOW!

They really liked heaven, and they all lived happily ever after.

God's Favorite Recipe:

PEANUT DREAMS

2/3 cup	peanut butter
3 Tbl	honey
1/4 cup	chopped nuts
1/4 cup	wheat germ
1/2 cup	coconut
2/3 cup	oats
3 Tbl	powdered milk
3 Tbl	water

Mix all the ingredients except the water in a large bowl. Slowly add the water and mix again. Take lumps about the size of your big toe, roll them into balls, and roll the balls in extra oats, wheat germ, coconut, or nuts. Put the balls onto a plate and place into the refrigerator for an hour.

After you share some with your family and friends, keep the rest refrigerated for another time.